MW01285722
read it - love it - return it

In My Opinion

by Deb Bird
Illustrated by Josh Alves

To all of the Maddies out
there who have wonderful
opinions and are excited
to share them.

Hi! My name is
Maddie and in my
opinion my ideas are
always the best.

Like the time Mom asked me if
I would rather get the
green polka dot dress
or the
pink fluffy one.

Of course the pink one – I feel like a princess when I wear it.

But my brother Jacob says I look
like a giraffe in a Tutu!

That's just his
SILLY opinion.

Or when Dad asked if
we should have
ice cream
or
pudding
for dessert.

Cookie Dough ice cream of course!
So chewy and delicious!

But Jacob said pudding
because it's so smooth!
What?!

That's just his
OUTRAGEOUS opinion.

And remember when my teacher
asked if we would rather color with

colored pencils

or

markers.

Oh, I love to color with colored pencils
because it's so easy to stay inside the lines!

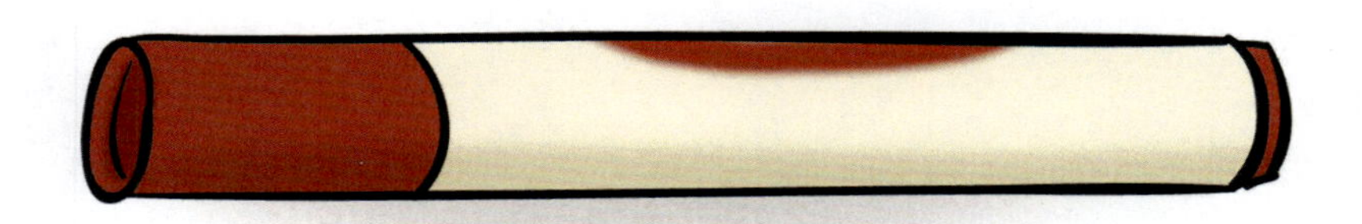

But Brady said markers cause they're so bright and everyone else said, "Yeah... markers!"

Well, that was just their **CRAZY** opinion.

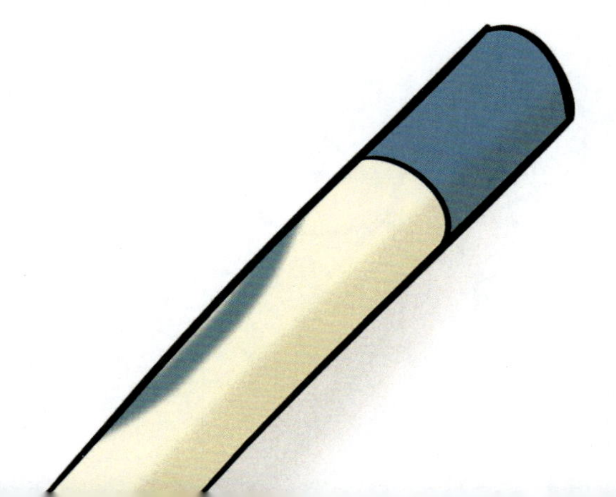

Our teacher wants us to write a story about our favorite season.

Well why didn't she just say,
"Write about summer", cause everyone knows summer is the best. Swimming, biking, going to the park...

Wait a minute...
Alex is writing about winter...
What can she possibly say
about winter?

That's just her **PERSONAL** opinion!

At recess, Maggie asked me if I wanted to play jump rope or swing. I said, "Swing, of course". I love to go up high and make believe I'm an astronaut flying through space...

But Anna said she wanted to
jump rope because she learned a new
song that helps her to jump 10 times.

Ridiculous!

Sing a song when you can
be an astronaut!

Well, that's just her
WACKY opinion!

I know! I know! Yeah, Yeah, I got it! I'm so smart! This is something that we can all agree on... Yep, I did it, I found something you can't argue about!

Wait until you hear it!
Are you ready?
Hang onto your hat!

The Tooth Fairy is the best!
Yep, the Tooth Fairy
is the best!!!!

Or is she?

Deb Bird is a literacy teacher and lives on a lake in Orono Maine with her husband, Dean. Her writing inspiration comes from watching the children around her.

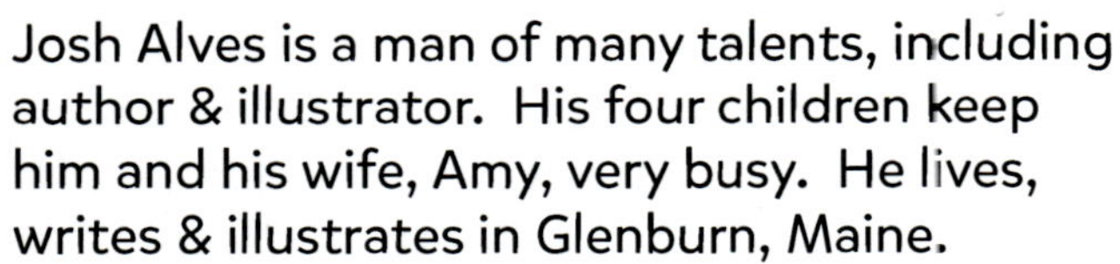

Josh Alves is a man of many talents, including author & illustrator. His four children keep him and his wife, Amy, very busy. He lives, writes & illustrates in Glenburn, Maine.

Maddie Healey loves to share her thoughts and opinions with her Mom, Dad, and two siblings, Jacob & Jenni. She attends school in Dover, New Hampshire. Her inspiration comes from...

Well, we're not really sure about that.

Made in the USA
Middletown, DE
06 May 2019